Pack a mug.

Pack a pin.

Pack It

Written by
Daisy Hawkins

Illustrated by
David Wilkerson

Published in 2026 by
Norwood House Press
2544 Clinton Street
Buffalo, NY 14224

Printed in the United States of America

Library of Congress Cataloging-in-Publication Data:
Names: Hawkins, Daisy, author. | Wilkerson, David, illustrator.
Title: Pack it / written by Daisy Hawkins, illustrated by David Wilkerson. Got it / by Daisy Hawkins.
Description: Buffalo, NY : Norwood House Press, 2026. | Series: Phonics all-stars: phase 2 |
Identifiers: ISBN 9781978577817 (pbk.) | ISBN 9781978577824 (library bound) | ISBN 9781978577831 (ebook)
Subjects: LCSH: Reading–Phonetic method–Juvenile literature. | English language--Phonetics–Juvenile literature. | Luggages–Packing–Juvenile literature. | Metal detectors–Juvenile literature.
Classification: LCC LB1573.3 H395 2026 | DDC 372.465–dc23

CPSIA compliance information: Batch #CW26NHP: For further information contact Norwood House Press at 1-800-237-9932.

Pack a top.

Pack a pet.

Pack a ten.

Pack a cap.

Got a pad and a pen?

Got It

By Daisy Hawkins

Get the stick.

Run it on the mud.

Get a rock.

Tip and tap the rock.

Got it!

Get a pan to the dock.

Pack mud into the pan.
Tip and tap the pan.

Got it!

Sid and Sam can get it.